This Journal Belongs To:

_____

_____

SUMMER SUMMER

ISBN-10: 1722379502

HOW TO USE THIS JOURNAL:

You don't have to go through the pages in order. Feel free to jump around.

There are prompts on each page to get you started, but YOU make the rules!

Write, doodle, draw, color or use stickers, pictures, tickets, maps, or anything

else that holds a memory to capture the moment.

Have Fun!

My Summer Bucket List

- ○ HAVE A LEMONADE STAND
- ○ PICK BERRIES
- ○ EAT POPSICLES
- ○ VISIT THE FARMERS MARKET
- ○ MAKE ICE CREAM
- ○ GO TO THE POOL
- ○ FLY KITES
- ○ WATCH FIREWORKS
- ○ GO TO A MUSEUM
- ○ RIDE A BICYCLE
- ○ VISIT THE ZOO
- ○ READ ALL DAY
- ○ GO CAMPING
- ○ HAVE A PICNIC

My Summer Bucket List

- ○
- ○
- ○
- ○
- ○
- ○
- ○
- ○
- ○
- ○
- ○
- ○
- ○

About ME

I am _____ years old.

I live in _____,

with _____.

This is the summer before _____ grade.

My friends are _____

_____

_____.

This summer, I look forward to _____

_____

_____.

My SELF Portrait

7

Location: _____

What I did today:

The weather was:

Rate the day:

I ♡

One thing that made me smile:

One thing I learned today:

Doodles and Pictures

What is the most important thing you would like to do this summer?

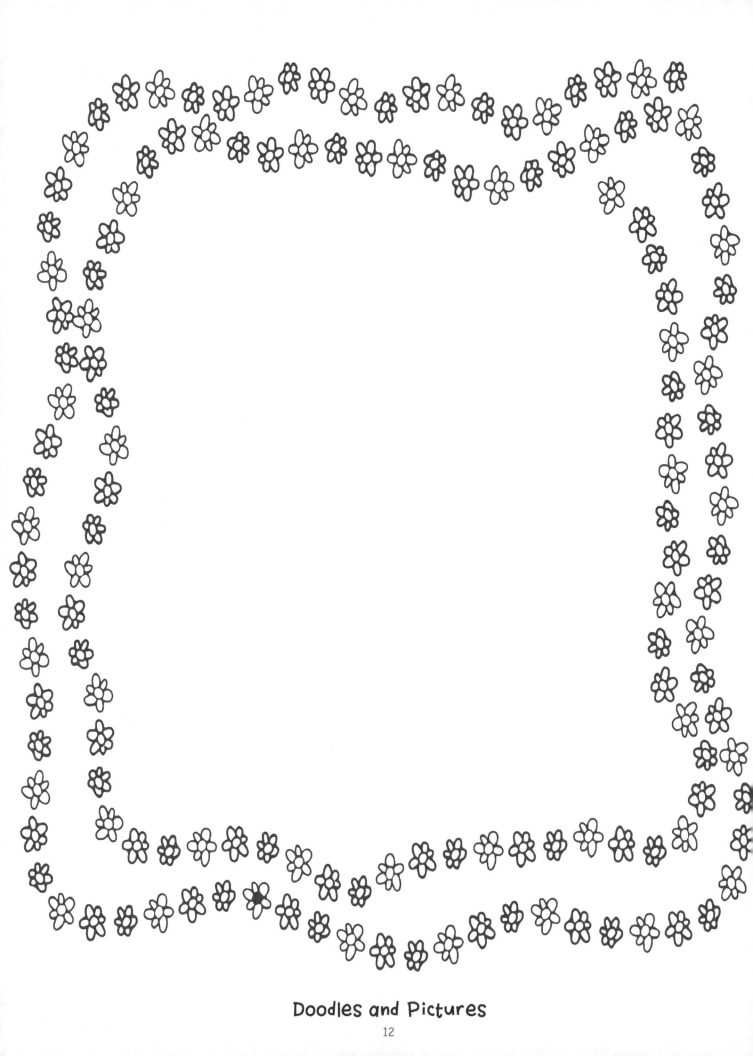

Doodles and Pictures

Location: _____

Date:

What I did today:

The weather was:

I 🤍

One thing I learned today:

One thing that made me smile:

Rate The Day:
⭐⭐⭐⭐⭐

Write about your ideal summer day.
What does it include?

Doodles and Pictures

Location: _____

What I did today:

The weather was:

I ♡

One thing I learned today:

One thing that made me smile:

Rate The Day:
☆ ☆ ☆ ☆ ☆

Write about a funny memory from a road trip.

_____

_____

_____

_____

_____

_____

_____

_____

_____

_____

_____

Location: _____

What I did today:

The weather was:

Rate the day:

I ♡

One thing that made me smile:

One thing I learned today:

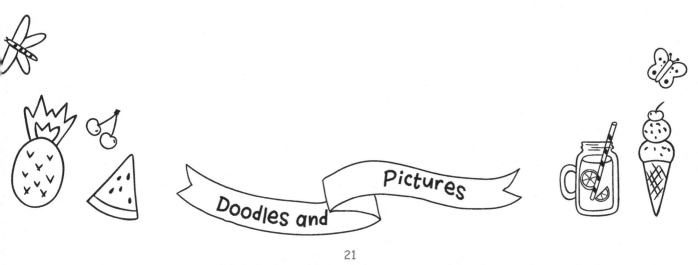

Doodles and Pictures

The Ultimate Lemonade Stand

We Need:

- [ ] Lemonade
- [ ] Cups
- [ ] Ice
- [ ] Table
- [ ]
- [ ]
- [ ]
- [ ]

Location:

Friends To Invite:

- [ ]
- [ ]
- [ ]
- [ ]
- [ ]
- [ ]
- [ ]
- [ ]

Notes:

_____

_____

_____

How to make LEMONADE....

First,

Next,

Then,

Last,

LEMONADE

INGREDIENTS

Item	Amount
_____	_____
_____	_____
_____	_____
_____	_____
_____	_____
_____	_____

Location: _____

What I did today:

The weather was:

Rate the day:

I ♡

One thing that made me smile:

One thing I learned today:

Doodles and Pictures

Write about a day at the pool or the beach.

Doodles and Pictures

Location: _____

Date:

What I did today:

The weather was:

I ♡

One thing I learned today:

One thing that made me smile:

Rate The Day:

What is your favorite summer holiday? Why?

How does your family celebrate it?

Doodles and Pictures

Location: _____

Date:

What I did today:

The weather was:

I ♡

One thing I learned today:

One thing that made me smile:

Rate The Day:

Write about your family picnic or backyard BBQ.

Location: _____

What I did today:

The weather was:

Rate the day:

I ♡

One thing that made me smile:

One thing I learned today:

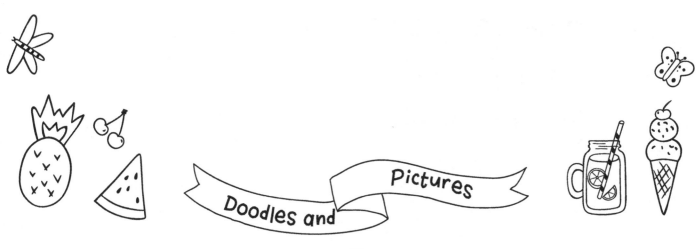

Doodles and Pictures

If I invented an ICE CREAM flavor.....

Flavor Name:

Tastes Like:

Ingredients:

☐

☐

☐

☐

☐

☐

It would be best served as:

☐ A scoop on a cone   ☐ Ice Cream Sandwich

☐ Ice Cream Sundae   ☐

☐ Ice Cream Float   ☐

DELICIOUS

SWEET

ICE ♡ CREAM

Location: _____

Date:

What I did today:

The weather was:

Rate the day:

I ♡

One thing that made me smile:

One thing I learned today:

42

Doodles and Pictures

Let's Chat!

Tell me your favorite thing to do.

Where is your favorite place to go?

What do you want to be when you grow up?

What is something you don't like:

What is your favorite food to eat?

What is your favorite game?

Date:_____

45

Let's Chat!

Tell me your favorite summer activity?

What is your favorite book?

What do you like to do on a rainy day?

What is something you are good at?

What is your favorite food?

What is your favorite subject in school?

Date:_____

What is your earliest summer memory?

What is your favorite movie?

What do you dream about?

Date:_____

How to make ....

First, _____

_____

Next, _____

_____

_____

Then, _____

_____

Last, _____

_____

_____

Write the recipe for a favorite summer treat that your family makes.

INGREDIENTS

Item	Amount
_____	_____
_____	_____
_____	_____
_____	_____
_____	_____
_____	_____
_____	_____

How to make ....

First,

Next,

Then,

Last,

Write the recipe for a favorite summer treat that your family makes.

INGREDIENTS

Item	Amount
_____	_____
_____	_____
_____	_____
_____	_____
_____	_____
_____	_____
_____	_____

How to make ....

First, _____

_____

_____

Next, _____

_____

_____

Then, _____

_____

_____

Last, _____

_____

_____

Write the recipe for a favorite summer treat that your family makes.

INGREDIENTS

Item	Amount
_____	_____
_____	_____
_____	_____
_____	_____
_____	_____
_____	_____
_____	_____

Doodles and Pictures

Location: _____

Date:

What I did today:

The weather was:

I ♥

One thing I learned today:

Rate The Day:

☆☆☆☆☆

One thing that made me smile:

What would you show to a visitor coming to your town this summer?

Doodles and Pictures

Location: _____

What I did today:

The weather was:

I ♥

One thing I learned today:

One thing that made me smile:

Rate The Day:
☆☆☆☆☆

Location: _____

What I did today:

The weather was:

Rate the day:

I ♡

One thing that made me smile:

One thing I learned today:

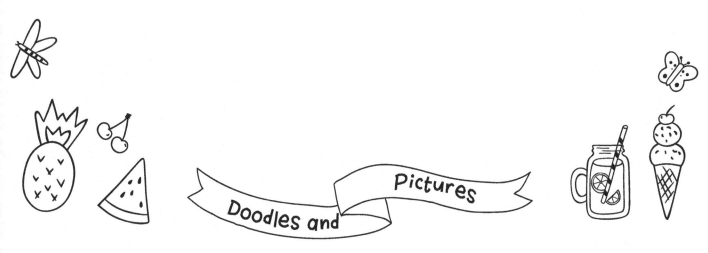

Doodles and Pictures

Imagine you are going on an adventure far away from home.

Where would you like to go?

☐
☐
☐
☐
☐

What will you see?

☐
☐
☐
☐
☐

Location: _____

What I did today:

The weather was:

Rate the day:

I 🤍

One thing that made me smile:

One thing I learned today:

Doodles and Pictures

You are going on vacation. Decide on a destination.

Where will you go?

How will you get there?

Make a list of things you want to do and places to see.

Things To Do

Places To See

☐

☐

☐

☐

☐

☐

☐

☐

Make a list of important things you need to pack.

☐

☐

☐

☐

☐

☐

☐

☐

Doodles and Pictures

Location: _____

Date:

What I did today:

The weather was:

I ♡

One thing I learned today:

One thing that made me smile:

Rate The Day:
☆ ☆ ☆ ☆ ☆

Write about your last visit to the zoo or a farm.

What animals did you see?

What new animals do you hope to see on a future visit?

Doodles and Pictures

Location: _____

What I did today:

The weather was:

I ♡

One thing I learned today:

One thing that made me smile:

Rate The Day:
☆☆☆☆☆

75

Write about a summer party you attended with your family.

Location: _____

Date:

What I did today:

The weather was:

Rate the day:

I ♡

One thing that made me smile:

One thing I learned today:

78

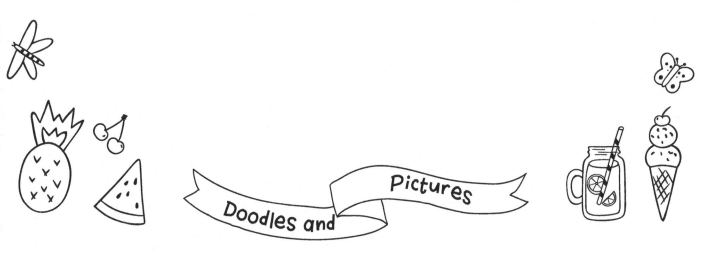

Doodles and Pictures

Free Space

Location: _____

What I did today:

The weather was:

Rate the day:

I ♡

One thing that made me smile:

One thing I learned today:

Doodles and Pictures

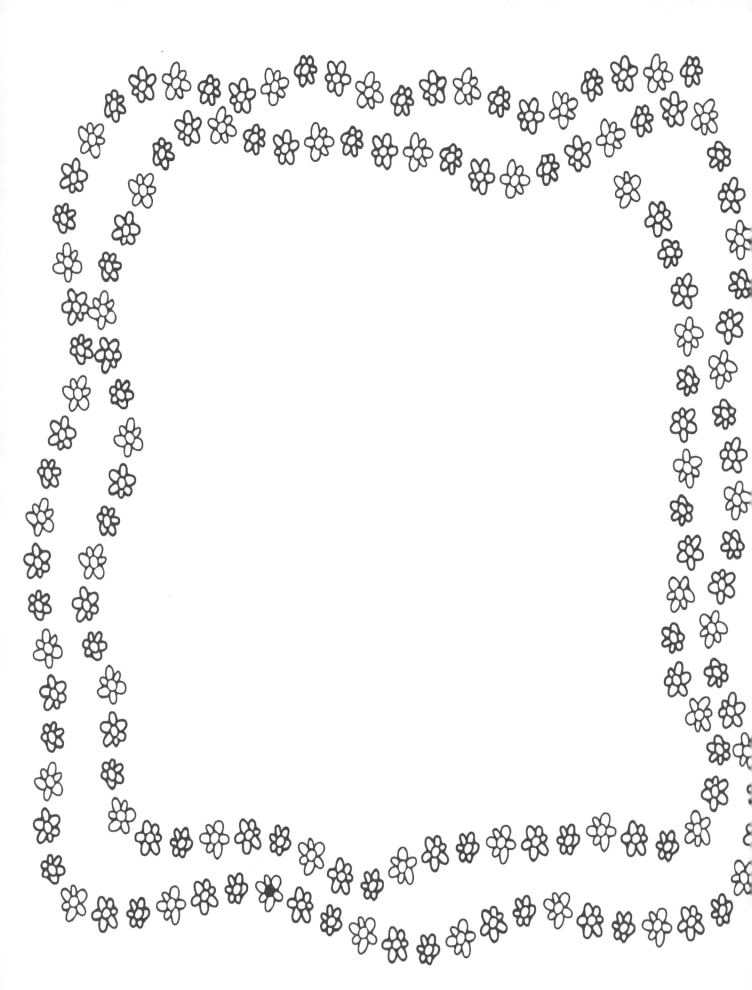

Doodles and Pictures

Location: _____

Date:

What I did today:

The weather was:

I ♥

One thing I learned today:

One thing that made me smile:

Rate The Day:
☆☆☆☆☆

87

Free Space

Doodles and Pictures

Location: _____

Date:

What I did today:

The weather was:

I ♥

One thing I learned today:

One thing that made me smile:

Rate The Day:
☆☆☆☆☆

Date:

What I did today:

The weather was:

Rate the day:

I ♡

One thing that made me smile:

One thing I learned today:

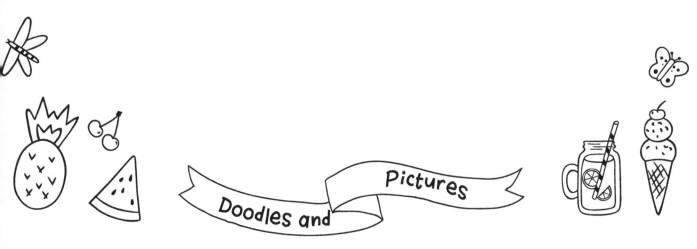

Doodles and Pictures

Free Space

Free Space

Free Space

MAIL

5¢ SPECIAL DELIVERY

Post Card

To:

Dear

Write to a teacher.

MAIL

5¢ SPECIAL DELIVERY

Post Card

To:

Dear _____

Write to a friend.

MAIL

5¢ SPECIAL DELIVERY

Post Card

To:

Dear _____

Write to someone you miss.

Post Card

To:

Dear _____

5¢ SPECIAL DELIVERY

To:

Post Card

Dear _____

SUMMER Reading iS FUN!

SUMMER READING CHALLENGE!

I read 20 minutes a day....

ON MY BED ☐	IN THE CAR ☐	AT THE BEACH ☐	WITH A FLASHLIGHT ☐
ON THE SOFA ☐	IN THE SUN ☐	BY THE POOL ☐	WITH A FRIEND ☐
IN MY BACKYARD ☐	IN A SILLY VOICE ☐	AT THE PARK ☐	AT THE LIBRARY ☐
AT THE MUSEUM ☐	TO A PARENT ☐	AS A FAMILY ☐	UNDER A TREE ☐

Color-in the box once you complete each challenge.

What is your favorite book this summer?

What is it about?

Who are the main characters?

SUMMER
READING LOG

Book Title	Author	Opinion Loved Liked Bored

The best of my Summer Memories

Funniest thing that happened:

_____

_____

_____

My most favorite part of this summer was:

_____

_____

_____

I had lots of FUN:

_____

_____

MY FAVORITES this summer were:

Ice Cream Flavor: _____

Food: _____

Book: _____

Color: _____

Song: _____

Movie: _____

Game: _____

Sport: _____

Place: _____

Activity: _____